GETTING FREE

Bert Ghezzi and Peter Williamson
General Editors

Getting Free

*How Christians Can Conquer
the Flesh and Overcome
Persistent Personal Problems*

Bert Ghezzi

SERVANT BOOKS
Ann Arbor, Michigan

Published by Servant Books
P.O. Box 8617
Ann Arbor, Michigan 48107

Cover Photo by John B. Leidy © 1982 Servant
Publications
Book Design by John B. Leidy

Scripture quotations are from the *Revised Standard
Version* of the Bible, copyrighted 1946, 1952 © 1971,
1973 and from the *New American Bible*, copyright
© 1970 by the Confraternity of Christian Doctrine,
Washington, D.C., all rights reserved.

Printed in the United States of America.
ISBN 0-89283-117-0

Contents

Living as a Christian

IN HUMAN TERMS, it is not easy to decide to follow Jesus Christ and to live our lives as Christians. Jesus requires that we surrender our selves to him, relinquish our aspirations for our lives, and submit our will to God. Men and women have never been able to do this easily; if we could, we wouldn't need a savior.

Once we accept the invitation and decide to follow Jesus, a new set of obstacles and problems asserts itself. We find that we are often ignorant about what God wants of us as his sons and daughters. For example, what does it mean practically to obey the first commandment—to love God with our whole mind, heart, and strength? How can we know God's will? How do we love people we don't like? How does being a Christian affect what we do with our time and money? What does it mean "to turn the other cheek?" In these areas—and many others—it is not easy to understand exactly what God wants.

Even when we do know what God wants, it can be quite difficult to apply his teaching to our daily lives. Questions abound. How do we find time to pray regularly? How do we repair a relationship with someone we have wronged or who has wronged us? How do we handle unruly emotional reactions? These are examples of perplexing questions about the application of Christian teaching to our daily lives.

Furthermore, we soon discover that Christians have enemies—the devil outside and the flesh within. Satan tempts us to sin; our inner urges welcome the temptation, and we find our will to resist steadily eroding.

Finally, we must overcome the world. We are living in an environment that is hostile toward what Christians believe and how they live, and friendly toward those who believe and do the opposite. The world in which we live works on our Christian resolve in many subtle ways. How much easier it is to think and act like those around us! How do we persevere?

There is a two-fold answer to these questions: To live successfully as Christians, we need both grace and wisdom. Both are freely available from the Lord to those who seek him.

As Christians we live by grace. The very life of God works in us as we try to understand God's teaching, apply it to our lives, and overcome the forces that would turn us aside from our chosen path. We always need grace, and grace is always there. The Lord is with us always, and the supply of his grace is inexhaustible.

Yet grace works with wisdom. Christians must *learn* a great deal about how to live according to God's will. We must study God's word in scripture, listen to Christian teaching, and reflect on our own experience and the experience of others. Many Christians today lack this kind of wisdom. This is the need which the *Living as a Christian* series is designed to meet.

The book you are reading is part of a series of books intended to help Christians apply the teaching of scripture to their lives. The authors of *Living as a Christian* books are pastoral leaders who have given this teaching in programs of Christian formation in various Christian communities. The teaching has stood the test of time. It has already helped many people grow as faithful servants of the Lord. We decided it was time to make this teaching available in book form.

All the *Living as a Christian* books seek to meet the following criteria:

- **Biblical.** The teaching is rooted in scripture. The authors and editors maintain that scripture is the word of God, and that it ought to determine what Christians believe and how they live.

- **Practical.** The purpose of the series is to offer down-to-earth advice about living as a Christian.

- **Relevant.** The teaching is aimed at the needs we encounter in our daily lives—at home, in school, on the job, in our day-to-day relationships.

- **Brief and Readable.** We have designed the series for busy people from a wide variety of backgrounds. Each of the authors presents profound Christian truths as simply and clearly as possible, and illustrates those truths by examples drawn from personal experience.

- **Integrated.** The books in the series comprise a unified curriculum on Christian living. They do not present differing views, but rather they take a consistent approach.

The format of the series makes it suitable for both individual and group use. The books in *Living as a Christian* can be used in such group settings as Sunday school classes, adult education programs, prayer groups, classes for teenagers, women's groups, and as a supplement to Bible study.

The *Living as a Christian* series is divided into several sets of books, each devoted to a different aspect of Christian living. These sets include books on Christian maturity, emotions in the Christian life, the fruit of the Holy Spirit, Christian personal relationships, Christian service, and, very likely, on other topics as well.

This book, *Getting Free,* is one of a set of books which will help you overcome obstacles to your growth in Christian maturity. Soon after making a serious commitment to the Lord, we usually become aware of things that hinder our growth—obstacles such as our own wrongdoing, the world, the flesh, and the devil. *Getting Free* and other books in this set present practical, scripturally based teaching that will help you overcome these barriers to growth in Christian maturity.

The editors dedicate the *Living as a Christian* series to Christian men and women everywhere who have counted the cost and decided to follow Jesus Christ as his disciples.

Bert Ghezzi and Peter Williamson
General Editors

Problems That Won't Quit

MY TWELVE-YEAR-OLD daughter, Elaine, loves horses. Recently she has been negotiating a trade with me—horseback riding lessons for violin. She does not know this, but my natural reaction against listening to violin exercises is a point in her favor. Of course horses are often the subject of conversation in our house. "Ruth's horse," I heard Elaine telling her mother, "is seven-eighths Arabian, I think." Just then a brother passed through the kitchen. Perfectly imitating her tone and cadence, he chirped wickedly, "Elaine is seven-eighths shrimp, I think." My poor wife laughed before she could catch herself.

Teasing of this sort has been a common problem in my family. The young man who delivered the above-quoted line is a master of the art. He seems to be made of the stuff that produces the likes of Bob Hope, those who are famous for dropping negative, though outrageously funny, one-liners. Our local stand-up comedian, however, after many lectures and some parental applause—clapping one flat stick against child's posterior—has come to regard his teasing as a problem. He has resolved a number of times to stop. Invariably, he has slipped and stung one of us. "I have a problem with teasing, don't I, Dad?" he asked me once. "Well, I try to stop, but I can't. I guess something in me keeps making me do it."

My son is not alone in his plight. Many Christians have problems they feel they cannot overcome. Sometimes their problems crop up after they've experienced a genuine spiritual renewal. What a terrible irony: to be filled with the Holy Spirit and to be plagued with apparently incurable problems! Is there a Christian who has not echoed my son's complaint: "I try to stop but something in me keeps making me do it?"

A Sampler of Problems

The problems Christians have fall into numerous categories. Most people have some emotional difficulties such as anger, self-condemnation, unruly desires, or fears. Many have faults or weaknesses in character that must change. And all are sinners. Consider the following real-life examples:

Example One: Anger and Anxiety. Tom and Sally, both active members of a community church, were married two years ago. As single people they had been regarded as model young Christian adults. Nonetheless, these fine young people had a very difficult time adjusting to married life. Major changes in a person's life, such as marriage, often flush out problems that have been hidden below the surface.

Sally, who had been very active in church groups, felt that Tom's desire for her to spend more time at home was selfish; it deprived her of her ministry. In addition, Tom's tendency to make snap decisions and his constant, low-level irritability made Sally fearful for their future relationship. It didn't take long before her worries swelled into full-fledged anxiety.

Tom had always been a little capricious. He had a long-standing problem with irritability (ask his mother). He interpreted Sally's difficulty with his impulsive decision-making as unwarranted criticism. He felt pressured by her resistance to his desire for her to stay at home more. As a result, his irritability grew worse until it sparked frequent arguments between them.

Tom and Sally knew they had problems. They both tried to stop. Neither could. Something seemed to prevent them from changing.

Tom's irritability and Sally's anxiety are examples of emotional problems. Modern Christians seem to have more problems with their emotions than Christians of earlier, say for example New Testament, times. Our functionalized society compels us to place a very high value on intimacy, and feelings are among our most intimate parts. Our whole environment prepares us to pay exquisite attention to how we feel. But the more attention we pay to our emotions the more problems we find—or make—for ourselves. Do not misunderstand. As Christians, we shouldn't model ourselves on stoics, striving to be free from our feelings. We should model ourselves on Jesus and his disciples instead. We should try to do everything *with* feeling: to get angry, cry at funerals, leap for joy. But the modern tendency to *follow after* feelings creates a host of problems for us.

Example Two: Addictions. All of us probably know someone who has struggled to be free of alcohol or drug addiction. Another, more subtle addiction, and one that afflicts contemporary Christians, is the TV habit. Jack, an insurance salesman, father of three, and faithful member of a Christian men's service group, is one such TV addict. In the past year he has developed the habit of turning on the set whenever his wife is upstairs nursing the baby. At times, he has become hooked by some utterly mindless show, spending up to two hours hypnotized by the electronic box.

His wife has begun to miss the few private times they had together. But Jack doesn't seem able to divorce himself from his new pastime.

Jack's TV habit may seem harmless enough. But in reality it is the kind of attachment that borders on idolatry. Habitual dependency on the media, food, sex, or anything else usually involves a degree of devotion that is improper. What seems innocent may, at root, border on serious wrongdoing. In Jack's case his seemingly harmless addiction may soon result in broken relationships with his wife and family.

Example Three: Curiosity. Mary works as a receptionist for the local county social service office for family counseling. Her job gives her access to confidential files that detail cases being handled by the bureau's counselors. Mary needs to handle the files, but rarely does any assignment require her to delve into them. But delve into them she does.

Ever since she was a child, Mary has been very curious about the personal lives of others. She has been reading other people's letters since she was about fifteen years old. Now she feels an inner drive to explore the files at work; the more she indulges the desire the more it seems to grow. Mary is a Christian who takes her faith to heart, but curiosity is a big problem for her. She has sought the advice of her pastor, but, as yet, she has not overcome her problem.

Mary's curiosity is a disorderly desire. It may have its root in some serious sin such as envy or pride. And it may lead to serious wrongdoing such as deceit (covering her tracks) or slander (telling others what she has discovered). Inability to control such tendencies is a fairly typical problem for Christians.

Example Four: Sexual Fantasies. Mark is the art director for an advertising agency. He and his wife Anne lead part of a Christian marriage enrichment program. The periodicals he must consult for his artwork often contain suggestive photos: he knows he lingers over them. Now and then, on business trips, he indulges his desire to spend an evening alone in his motel room reading a pornographic magazine. For several years now, his mind has been full of sexual fantasies.

Mark occasionally rationalizes his behavior to himself, pretending that his mental promiscuity enhances his sexual relationship with Anne. But in more objective moments, he admits this isn't true. Moreover, since his meditations frequently result in masturbation, he has not persuaded himself that the fantasies are all right. Mark thinks he has a problem that he'll never get rid of.

Sexual desire in itself is not a problem—it is the Creator's gift, planted in us to bind us to his purposes for humanity. Sexual desire is good. Nor are sexual temptations (even the most explicitly pornographic ones) exactly problems, unless we let them take control. Sexual temptations, like any temptation, are desires to do something God has outlawed. They might be difficult to resist and we might call the struggle a problem, but the sexual temptation itself is not the problem—our response is.

When do sexual thoughts become sin? A Roman Catholic priest once asked a young man in the confessional, "Have you been entertaining any impure thoughts lately?" The young man responded, "Oh, no, Father, but they sure have been entertaining me!" Sexual thoughts are only wrong if we indulge them, letting them entertain us with vicarious sexual pleasures. Every Christian must handle sexual desires. For many, at one time or other, they become the beginning of a problem.

An Inventory of Common Problems

In a number of places, the New Testament lists serious problems that stem from the flesh. If we are not impressed by these lists, we ought to be. They are not directed to pagans, but to Christians. The Lord knew that his children would be tempted to sin, so he warned us in advance:

> Now the works of the flesh are plain: fornication, impurity, licentiousness, idolatry, sorcery, enmity, strife, jealousy, anger, selfishness, dissension, party spirit, envy, drunkenness, carousing, and the like. I warn you, as I warned you before, that those who do such things shall not inherit the kingdom of God.
>
> (Gal 5:19-21)

The Bible presents such lists not to crush us, but to put us on the alert. We often feel trapped by our problems, but the Lord wants us to know that help is at hand.

Below is an expanded, contemporary list of problems Christians face. I expect that most readers will be familiar with these to some extent in their own lives.

addiction (alcohol, drugs, food, media, sex)
adultery (including lusting after a person in one's heart and getting into "spiritual friendships" that contradict commitments to be married or single)

ambition (self-seeking, putting our interests
    first)
anger (out of control, repressed, or expressed in
    a sinful way)
arrogance
bitterness (holding grudges, refusing to forgive)
boredom
cheating
competitiveness (always opposing oneself
    against others)
contentiousness
covetousness
criticalness
curiosity (prying, being a busybody)
depression
despair (giving up on God or oneself)
disloyalty
doubt (about God, others, oneself)
drunkenness (and getting high on drugs)
envy
fantasy (daydreaming, losing touch with reality,
    committing vicarious sin)
fear
fights
gluttony (habitual over-eating)
gossip
guilt
hatred
homosexual behavior
idolatry (worshipping false gods)
independence (cutting oneself off from others,
    insisting on one's preferences
irresponsibility

irritability
jealousy
laziness
lust
manipulation
masturbation
materialism (attachment to things)
meanness (the opposite of generous, being cruel)
moodiness (following one's feelings)
negativity
overspirituality (avoiding human responsibility under the guise of being "spiritual")
pornography
possessiveness
premarital sex
presumption (failing to rely on God or having unrealistic confidence in oneself)
pride (always putting oneself first, making invidious comparisons)
profanity
quarrels
rebellion
revenge
self-condemnation
shyness
slander
suicidal tendencies
teasing
thievery
unreliability
vulgarity
worry

If you recognize some of these problems in your own life, don't be disheartened. All of us tend to feel bad about ourselves when we fail, but grief for wrongdoing is good only if it is based on our having offended God. Then we can turn away from our old behavior. Grief for grief's sake is itself an offense. Only repentance that leads to change pleases God.

Have you tried to change but failed? Are you like my son who cannot stop teasing: "Something in me keeps making me do it?" If you have problems that won't go away, the Lord has help for you. Scripture presents a way of getting free from such problems.

It is the goal of this book to set forth that strategy in very practical terms. In the next chapter we will discuss the most common approach that Christians take to problems—the one that never works.

TWO

Willpower Christianity

"WELL, SCRIPTURE SAYS that God helps those who help themselves," declared the older of two men, whose animated discussion was verging on argument. He hoped to win his point by appealing to authority. Some onlookers were embarrassed for the man, and others found themselves resisting the smiles that lurked on the edges of their lips. Everyone except the speaker seemed to know that the line appears nowhere in the Bible.

Seldom are serious Christians fooled by this bogus Bible verse. They instinctively recognize it as a worldly notion masquerading as spiritual wisdom. They see immediately that it bends men away from God, who saves us, towards self, which cannot save anyone. Yet, judging by our daily behavior, I would have to conclude that many serious Christians conduct their lives as though "God helps those who help themselves" were a cardinal, biblical directive.

Willpower Christianity is perhaps the most common approach to living the Christian life. Men and women come to know the Lord and experience his love for them in a personal way. They hear and understand his teaching, his commands, and his principles, and they eagerly embrace them. But they make a big mistake when they begin to apply them to their own lives. They engage their wills as the chief, if not sole, agent charged with getting their lives into order.

Consider again the examples cited in the first chapter. The men and women presented in these vignettes are serious about their Christianity. Some were born and raised in Christian families and later made an adult commitment to Christ. For example, Mary, who struggles with curiosity, cannot remember a time when she did not feel drawn to the Lord. She recalls with joy the high school retreat at which she openly committed herself to follow him. Others, like Tom and Sally, came to know the Lord as adults and have dedicated themselves to serving him. All of them want to please the Lord and live their lives in accord with his teaching. Each of them, however, seems to have adopted the willpower approach.

It must be said that some of them have had some measure of success with it. Hearing and understanding God, deciding to do what he wants, and charging the will to accomplish it can be somewhat effective. When Mark, the art director, heard on a renewal weekend that Christians should pray regularly, he decided the following Monday to begin a daily morning prayer time, which he has been faithful to ever since. His wife Anne once did a Bible study on hospitality, saw what generosity the Lord expects of us towards guests, and decided to set aside the reluctance she had toward opening her home for this service. Deciding was enough, for ever since Anne and Mark have graciously hosted a fairly continuous stream of guests.

But Mark and Anne, Tom and Sally, Mary and the others only got so far with willpower Christianity. A simple decision seemed to bring some areas right into line with the Lord's design for them. But, when their wills encountered resistance, they were stymied and failed to enact the decision. On what must seem to him to be innumerable occasions, Tom has decided to stop being irritable, but he has not been able to obey his own commands. Something resists. Mark is discouraged and sometimes ashamed of the inability of his willpower to keep him from indulging in sexual fantasies. Something resists. And so on. Thus, willpower Christianity, as popular as it is, has only limited effectiveness. Some things our will can push right into place. Others it cannot budge no matter how hard we try.

In his letter to the Romans, Paul describes the plight of the Christian who takes the willpower approach to his life.

I do not understand my own actions. For I do not do what I want, but I do the very thing I hate. Now if I do what I do not want, I agree that the law is good. So then it is no longer I that do it, but sin which dwells within me. For I know that nothing good dwells within me, that is, in my flesh. I can will what is right, but I cannot do it. For I do not do the good I want, but the evil I do not want is what I do. . . . So I find it to be a law that when I want to do right, evil lies close at hand. For I delight in the law of God, in my inmost self, but I see in my members another law at war with the law of my mind and making me captive to the law of sin which dwells in my members.

(Rom 7:15-19, 21-23)

There is no Christian who cannot identify with the struggle depicted in this passage. At one time or another we all attempt to accomplish by willpower what we could have *freely* received from the Lord by living the life of the Spirit.

For the law of the Spirit of life in Christ Jesus has set me free from the law of sin and death. For God has done what the law, weakened by the flesh, could not do. (Rom 8:2-3)

Man alone cannot apply the law to his life. Sheer willpower is not enough. When he understands God's requirements and tries to obey, he discovers there is more going on than the activity of his intellect and will. He encounters external obstacles. He finds resistance within. Not that he should be surprised to find it, for that resistance is inextricably bound up with himself.

The cartoon character Pogo used to say, "We

have met the enemy and they is us." In his contrast of life in the Spirit and life under the law, this is the reality Paul describes as "the law, weakened by the flesh." Willpower Christianity, or the law approach, is not enough, because it expects an individual human to overcome a set of obstacles that no mere human, or even a host of humans, could ever expect to master. This is a hard word in the contemporary age when self-reliance has become, even among Christians who should know better, the virtue par-excellence. Self-reliance is good, but it is no match for the hostility hurled at us by our enemy.

THREE

What We're Up Against

THE LAW APPROACH TO Christian living, while it cannot bring us into perfect conformity to the ways of God nor deliver us from all of our problems, has this particular advantage: it can demonstrate that the person is up against an enemy larger than himself—and that whatever it is, he cannot handle it on his own. Learning this truth is a valuable lesson. It is even worth a few bouts with self-reliance, if we learn it well.

Problems that I encounter in my Christian life may lead either to doom or deliverance. They lead to doom if I am overcome by them and succumb. However, problems can lead to deliverance, if I approach them properly. Every obstacle I encounter living as a Christian can be both an opportunity for grace, and a chance for me to acquire more wisdom about the enemy's operations.

Obstacles to Christian living stem from a complex of interrelated sources. None of them will submit to taming by mere human authority. Scripture describes them as mighty spiritual forces linked in a determined conspiracy to destroy

humanity. Their traditional names are the world,
the flesh, and the devil.

Lately, under the influence of modern styles of
thought, some Christians have carelessly lost a
healthy sense of fear in the face of these deadly
foes. We should not spurn the benefits of human
wisdom, but at the same time we dare not let
current intellectual fashions blind us to the
spiritual realities that God says will harm us if we
do not maintain the alert. What better way to
destroy us than to persuade us that sin, the world,
the flesh, and the devil are merely metaphysical
by-products of the primitive cultures in which
scripture was written, and certainly not real nor
dangerous? We might thus be lulled into surrender
without putting up a fight.

The World as Enemy

The world, as defined in scripture, is an
inhospitable place for humanity. Scripture declares that the world is opposed to the Father and
that friendship with the world makes a man an
enemy of God. "Do not love the world," wrote
John, "or the things in the world. If any one loves
the world, love for the Father is not in him. For all
that is in the world, the lust of the flesh and the lust
of the eyes and the pride of life, is not of the Father
but is of the world" (1 Jn 2:15-16). James is even
more pointed: "Do you not know that friendship
with the world is enmity with God? Therefore
whoever wishes to be a friend of the world makes

himself an enemy of God" (Jas 4:4). These are
hard words indeed for many contemporary
Christians. Some balk at the notion that the world
is an enemy because they mistakenly think that the
term refers to all of creation. But the same Creator
who warns us of the world has declared that all
that he made is *good*. The created world, then, is
not the enemy.

Some Christians, out of love for mankind,
dedicate themselves in generous service to im-
proving human conditions, but in the process
grow somewhat contemptuous of the idea that the
world is our enemy. These Christians would do
well to recover the traditional wariness of the
world. Otherwise, in the name of the second great
commandment, they may find themselves serving
under enemy banners. They are in danger of
becoming infatuated with a gospel whose primary
agenda has become a secularized one.

The "world," in the biblical warnings cited,
does not refer to creation or the natural realm. Nor
does it simply indicate the affairs of mankind,
human achievements, or humanitarianism. The
world which is inimical to man is unredeemed
human society, the aggregate of men and women
who do not serve the Lord. The world consists of
the relationships, practices, policies, and plans of
the millions who remain in bondage to the empire
of darkness, sin, and death. It is not a safe place for
Christians to walk unawares. It is an environment
that bends us away from God. We pick up its ways
unconsciously, through imitation, social influence,

education, and the media. For example, polls and studies indicate that Christians immersed in our contemporary secular environment conduct themselves no differently from non-Christians in matters such as abortion and premarital sex. Their behavior and opinions seem to be more influenced by peer pressure and the evening news than by the gospel of Christ or the church. They are like pedestrians walking on the next block when a parade passes by. Without even knowing it, they walk to the cadence of the drums.

The world is a significant source of the personal problems that many Christians experience. The conditions of our society are ideal for fostering emotional difficulties. The prevailing tone of conversation is often negative and critical. People seldom encourage one another, and they express little or no affection. At work or in groups, we have to watch out for people who might use us or climb over us to reach their goals. These patterns are the basic material from which problems with fear, insecurity, low self-esteem, and anxiety are woven.

The Sin Factor

The force at work in the world to turn men away from the Lord is sin. I do not mean sin simply as individual acts of wrongdoing, but sin as an objective, powerful force. Notice that this is the meaning of sin that Paul talks about in his letter to the Romans.

What then shall we say? That the law is sin? By
no means! Yet, if it had not been for the law, I
should not have known sin. I should not have
known what it is to covet if the law had not said,
"You shall not covet." But sin, finding opportunity in the commandment, wrought in me all
kinds of covetousness. Apart from the law sin
lies dead. I was once alive apart from the law,
but when the commandment came, sin revived
and I died; the very commandment which
promised life proved to be death to me. For sin,
finding opportunity in the commandment,
deceived me and by it killed me. (Rom 7:7-12)

Sin here is not merely a particular act of
covetousness. Nor is it merely the aggregation of
many acts of wrongdoing. Paul regards sin as an
objective condition. Sin is a reality that operates
on man—it takes advantage of the command-
ments, using them to destroy us. In this particular
case, sin, which Paul speaks of as a spiritual
substance, works on man like one of the Sirens in
Greek mythology, luring him by enchanted song
onto the rocks of wrongdoing and, ultimately,
death.

Sin sums up in itself the alienation of unredeemed humanity from God. Thus, it con-
stitutes a constant state of war, creature versus
Creator. This explains why mere human effort—
willpower Christianity on any scale—cannot
ultimately solve the problems we face. When a

veteran baseball player replaces the rookie who had committed three errors and then makes the game-losing error himself, his teammates complain that the rookie had so messed up left field that no one could have played it. The same sort of situation exists on a grander scale in the world. Sin has messed things up so much that we cannot straighten them out on our own power.

The Mastermind

We are not up against some accidental dislocation of our relationship with the Lord. The way that sin operates in the world is not haphazard. Scripture says that Satan, the self-declared enemy of God and man, masterminds the effort against God's work on the earth. "Your adversary the devil," warns Peter, "prowls around like a roaring lion, seeking some one to devour" (1 Pt 5:8). He addresses the Ephesians, saying, "You were dead through the trespasses and sins in which you once walked, following the course of this world, following the prince of the power of the air, the spirit that is now at work in the sons of disobedience. Among these we all once lived in the passions of our flesh, following the desires of body and mind, and so we were by nature children of wrath, like the rest of mankind" (Eph 2:1-3). John puts it succinctly: "We know that we are of God, and the whole world is in the power of the evil one" (1 Jn 5:19).

If we have carelessly allowed this personal

enemy to fade into some vague fog of impersonal evil forces, we should correct our mistake. The New Testament shows that Jesus' spiritual warfare was not a case of good versus evil, impersonal forces at war with one another, but God versus Satan. From the beginning of his ministry, Jesus exercised his Father's authority over personal evil spirits, calling demons by name and casting them out. In the end, Jesus, the sinless victim, conquered death, stripping power from Satan, his personal enemy.

The contemporary reduction of the devil to a legend is a clever ploy. What better way for the devil to catch humans off guard than to evaporate into the thin air of a theological discussion?

Satan is the architect of an empire of grand design that he has erected in opposition to the kingdom of God on the earth. He has assembled a vast army of his servants, both spiritual and human, and deployed them in manifold ways to achieve his purposes. He masterminds the whole world system, integrating the forces of sin and death. He and his hosts of fallen angels craftily spin webs of deceit to ensnare hapless humans, whom they hope to destroy. Temptations that shimmer with allurement and lies that seem to have the ring of truth are among his most effective weapons. Confusion, doubt, and anxiety are deadly arrows in his quiver. Satan, the would-be-mastermind of our doom, is an enemy not to be trifled with. No man on his own strength or will, except Jesus Christ himself, is any match for him.

The cross of Jesus Christ has assured Satan of his final defeat. Still, he lingers on, attempting by whatever means to take with him as many humans as he can into that defeat. Like a great spider, he would sting us into submission so that he might devour us at will. This in fact is the enemy's specific purpose for us. After the final summing up of human history, which Christians expect at the Second Coming, the devil will feed eternally on those people foolish enough to follow him.

The world, sin, and the devil have thrown uncountable, miserable obstacles in our paths. But before we blame them entirely for our problems, we must admit that something in us is inclined to collaborate with the enemy.

FOUR

The Fifth Column

WE HAVE FORMIDABLE external enemies. The problems Christians face daily are largely traceable to the activities of these enemies. But, if we are honest, we must admit that a considerable part of our problem comes from within ourselves. The world, sin, or the devil tantalize us into doing things we hate; they prevent us from obeying God's law and from molding our life according to his principles. But our experience tells us that something inside us collaborates with our enemies. Something within us opposes our desire to follow the Lord. We usually know what is right, and we generally hate what is wrong. What is it that makes us do the very things we hate? The word that some translations of scripture use to name this something is the *flesh*.

For those who live according to the flesh set their minds on the things of the flesh, but those who live according to the Spirit set their minds on the things of the Spirit. To set the mind on the flesh is death, but to set the mind on the Spirit is life and peace. For the mind that is set on the flesh is hostile to God; it does not submit to God's law, indeed it cannot; and those who are in the flesh cannot please God.

But you are not in the flesh, you are in the Spirit, if in fact the Spirit of God dwells in you.
(Rom 8:5-9)

For you were called to freedom, brethren; only do not use your freedom as an opportunity for the flesh, but through love be servants of one another. . . .

But I say, walk by the Spirit, and do not gratify the desires of the flesh. For the desires of the flesh are against the Spirit, and the desires of the Spirit are against the flesh; for these are opposed to each other, to prevent you from doing what you would.
(Gal 5:13, 16-17)

But I, brethren, could not address you as spiritual men, but as men of the flesh, as babes in Christ. I fed you with milk, not with solid food; for you were not ready for it; and even yet you are not ready, for you are still of the flesh. For while there is jealousy and strife among you, are you not of the flesh, and behaving like ordinary men? (1 Cor 3:1-3)

In each of these passages, the word *flesh* is used to name that element in us which prevents us from obeying God's law or involves us in some wrongdoing against others.

What the Flesh Is Not

When the New Testament names that within us which resists God's law, it uses the Greek word transliterated *sarx*. The literal meaning of *sarx* is "body," and sometimes the Bible uses the word in this sense. Also, in some translations the word *flesh* is used to refer simply to the human body. However, when the New Testament talks about our inner susceptibility to sin and terms it the *flesh*, we should understand that it is not talking about our physical body. The New Testament teaches that the flesh, not the body, leads us to sin.

That the flesh operates in our intellect confirms this fact. Galatians, chapter 5, catalogues the works of the flesh: immorality, impurity, licentiousness, idolatry, sorcery, enmity, strife, jealousy, anger, selfishness, dissension, party spirit, envy, drunkenness, and carousing. All of these, including those with an emotional or sexual component, are based in our mind. Jesus himself taught that "what comes out of the mouth proceeds from the heart, and this defiles a man. For out of the heart come evil thoughts, murder, adultery, fornication, theft, false witness, slander" (Mt 15:18-19). It isn't the physical body that tempts us to such wrongdoing, but the flesh, working in our thoughts and desires.

Christians frequently confuse the flesh with sexuality. However, when the New Testament teaches about the flesh it does not equate it with sexual desire. This is not to say that the flesh does not seduce us into sexual sin. It can work to distort our sexuality, but the flesh is not itself identical with sexual desire. Sex can work properly in the Christian life, but the "flesh" Paul speaks of never can. God gave men and women sexual desire so that they could cooperate with him in establishing new families as building blocks in the new humanity. Used within the bounds the Lord set for it, sexuality leads not to sin but to good. By exercising vigilance and wisdom, Christians can prevent the flesh from manipulating them into sexual expressions unacceptable to the Lord.

The New Testament does not equate the flesh with our emotions, either. This is an easy mistake for Christians to make in a culture where the focus on feelings has expanded to near delirium. Even though the flesh is distinct from emotions, it may play a big part in a person's emotional difficulties. In the case studies presented in the first chapter, Tom's irritability, Sally's anxiety, and Mary's curiosity all constitute emotional problems which have been strongly influenced by the work of the flesh.

If the flesh isn't the body, sexual desire, nor the emotions, what is this thing within us that makes us so susceptible to sin?

The Fifth Column

Let me borrow an analogy from modern warfare to help us understand the nature of the flesh. At the very end of the Spanish Civil War, itself a prelude to World War II, the city of Madrid was the last stronghold of loyalist republican forces, who opposed the armies of General Franco. Four columns of troops marched against the beleagured city and Franco's forces prevailed. According to journalists who reported on the battle, its conquest was assured by the existence of a "fifth column" *inside* the city walls, which worked to lay it open to the approaching enemy. "Fifth column" has come to mean an enemy within that collaborates with external enemies. The fifth column makes contact with the advancing enemy, takes up its cause within the city, throws the gates open to attack, and aids in the assault that produces defeat.

The New Testament describes the flesh as a fifth column operating within us to bring us under the influence of our external enemies. Sin is at work in the world around us, an enemy out to conquer us. We would be much less vulnerable to its advances were it not that the flesh works on us from within, making contact with sin. The flesh takes up sin's cause by persuading us that it is attractive, even irresistible. The flesh throws open our defenses and escorts the enemy inside. This enemy within connects with the enemy without. The fruit of their union is an act of wrongdoing or a problem that can correctly be called a work of the flesh.

In Tolkien's *The Two Towers*, King Theoden and his entire kingdom have been reduced to near impotence by the influence of Wormtongue, a traitorous advisor actually in the service of an enemy. This enemy within has eroded the courage and hope of the aging king and nearly persuaded him to turn away the aid and counsel that comes through the wizard Gandalf and his companions. When we set our mind on the flesh, it provides the same kind of direction for us that Wormtongue did for Theoden. The flesh opposes aid and counsel, grace and teaching from God. "For the desires of the flesh are against the Spirit, and the desires of the Spirit are against the flesh; for these are opposed to each other, to prevent you from doing what you would" (Gal 5:17).

The Old Man

The flesh can also be understood as a collection of evil tendencies at work within us. These wicked inclinations are the heritage we have from the "old man." Paul uses this term to refer to our participation in the unredeemed nature of fallen man. We all recognize the old man by his bent—he is turned away from God; he is inclined to evil and evil is inclined to him; he is always ready for some mischief, never tiring, never satisfied. Weak in the face of sin's allurements, he is strong, even stubborn, when it comes to resisting correction. Service and obedience are words beyond his comprehension. His one goal in life is self-fulfillment. That's a word the old man understands.

Paul tells the Colossians that they have "put off

the old nature with its practices and have put on the new nature, which is being renewed in knowledge after the image of its creator" (Col 3:9-10). Literally, Paul says that they have put off the old man and put on the new man. But traces of the old man must have remained alive and active in the Colossians, since, in this same passage, Paul commands them to put a stop to sins of the flesh: immorality, impurity, anger, malice, slander, and foul talk.

The old man is persistent. Even when we have put him off and put on Christ, his evil tendencies continue to influence us. He hangs around, and we must keep repeating the process. Paul directs the Ephesians to put off the old man and put on the new man, even though they had been Christians long enough to have expected their old man to be thoroughly dead. "Put off your old nature [man] which belongs to your former manner of life and is corrupt through deceitful lusts, and be renewed in the spirit of your minds, and put on the new nature [man], created after the likeness of God in true righteousness and holiness" (Eph 4:22-23). The flesh is the residue of the old man in us. He lingers on, to cause us problems—if we let him.

FIVE

Release from Our Enemies

WITH SO GREAT a swarm of enemies threatening us, it is no wonder that we say "Amen" to the exasperated plea of the Christian in Romans, chapter 7: "Wretched man that I am! Who will deliver me from this body of death?" (7:24). Mercifully, Paul does not allow the question to go unanswered. "Thanks be to God through Jesus Christ our Lord!" he says.

Paul does not present the human condition depicted in Romans, chapter 7, as an incurable, terminal disease. The Lord who delivered us from the bondage of sin and death will also save us in our life. He has already intervened mightily by sending Jesus to alter the once fatal destiny of humans. He continues to intervene, defending us against our external enemies and freeing us from the treason of the enemy within.

The Work of Christ

God's original plan in creation was to have sons and daughters fashioned in his own image and likeness. They were to know him, love him, and

live in close communion with him, sharing his own
life. Tempted by Satan, the Lord's personal
enemy, they traded the freedom of this union for
enslavement to the empire of darkness. In place of
eternal life, Satan gave them death; for holiness,
he gave them sin. Their constant hunger for God,
a hunger they had been born with, could never be
satisfied. Rather, they found themselves in the
service of a counterfeit god whose purpose was to
devour them.

In spite of their treasonable behavior, the Lord
maintained his determination to have a race of
men and women in his own image and likeness. He
sent the Second Person of the Godhead, his only
Son, Jesus Christ, to establish a new humanity.
God himself became a man—embodying the
human condition, weakness and all (except for
sin). While Jesus lived on earth he assembled a
community of men and women who would be the
first to become part of the new humanity. And he
waged war against Satan and his armies.

The climactic act of his earthly ministry
conquered the enemy and founded the new
humanity. The Sinless One took all sin upon
himself and freely submitted to death by crucifixion. But, to his shock, Satan could not hold the
Lord in death. For Jesus had no sin, and sin was
the enemy's only hold on mankind. Thus Jesus
defeated the ancient enemy. He broke open the
gates of darkness and despoiled hell of its captives.
They became in that moment the heavenward side
of the new human race.

The Holy Spirit breathed new life into Jesus and he burst from the grave. The New Man returned to his Father's side. From there he poured out on all his followers the very same Holy Spirit who raised him alive from the grave. They were the new humanity on the earth, now charged with incorporating all men and women into their communion.

The work of Christ was twofold. By his death and resurrection he conquered Satan, sin, and death—man's mortal enemies. He also became the Second Adam, the head and founder of a new humanity, the church.

The Work of the Holy Spirit

The Holy Spirit raised Jesus from the dead. He conferred new life on the head of the new humanity and conferred that same new life on the new humanity itself. The Holy Spirit is the presence of God dwelling in the members of the new human race. He draws Christian men and women into the very life of the Trinity. His presence within them makes them holy just as his presence made holy the Temple of Israel. By his manifold gifts, the Holy Spirit equips men and women to build the Christian community according to the mind of God. He is the source of the power that animates and strengthens the followers of Christ for their service. His actions make Christians more like God. He transforms the members of the new humanity so that they grow more perfectly into the image and likeness of the New Man. However, before they can be imprinted with the character of Christ, his followers must be free from the enemy within.

The Holy Spirit delivers Christians from the flesh and its effects by leading them to surrender to Christ and by providing them with an alternative principle for living. Loosed from the fleshly influences that bent them away from God, Christians are free to live their life in obedience to the Lord. As they do, day by day, their character becomes more like God's—marked by love, joy, peace, patience, kindness, goodness, reliability, generosity, self-control, and the like. So the Holy Spirit empowers the new humanity with new life and produces the *character* of the New Man, Jesus Christ, in his brothers and sisters.

Release from our enemies is the result of the work of Christ and of the Holy Spirit. Jesus frees us from Satan, sin, and death. The Holy Spirit frees us from the grip of the flesh and its effects on us. Jesus and the Holy Spirit have conquered for us, but, if we refuse their power and renounce their methods, we place ourselves in jeopardy. If we insist on self-reliance, on our own strength and strategies, our foes can still do us real harm. We must *appropriate* our Christian freedom. Otherwise, despite victories and broken chains, we will behave like men and women in bondage. To maintain Christ's conquest of Satan and his kingdom, we must master the Lord's strategy and tactics and become adept at using the weapons he gave us. In short, we must wage spiritual warfare.

The New Humanity

The Lord established the new humanity itself as the chief antidote to the world and sin. Christian community is an alternative environment to that of the world, which is hostile to God and bends his people away from him. Members of the new race orient everything in their lives to serving God and loving one another. In the Christian community they are integrated into a set of relationships where they find mutual commitment, care, and service. In churches, groups, and communities where attention is paid to relationship-building, Christians are living lives relatively free of the world's influences, though not without a struggle. But if churches and groups fail to build a Christian environment, the world will encroach upon them with ease and their members will find no release from its bent.

The new humanity is against the world for the world's own sake. Christian community is against the world in obedience to the Lord's direction that we not love the world, since those who love the world place themselves at enmity with the Father. Practically speaking, Christians implement this directive by patterning their everyday life on the teaching of scripture. This will mean that the new humanity will build a Christian subculture, radically different from the dominant culture of the world. Within that subculture, men and women can become what the Lord intended them to be. If we fail to be "against the world," if we build no alternative Christian culture, men and women of God will walk, talk, think, act, live, and die not in God's ways, but in the ways of those who do not follow him.

Christian community is "for the world" because the Lord loves the men and women who are trapped in the world system. He wants to incorporate them into the new humanity. To be "for the world" our churches and groups should be characterized by openness and growth. They should be hospitable places that welcome and involve newcomers cheerfully and warmly. The Lord has charged Christians to be his messengers of rescue to the world. Evangelism, not judgment, must be our watchword. The church must be tirelessly busy introducing people to the Lord and to the community of redeemed men and women.

In the warfare against Satan, the Lord has personally won the decisive battle. He has pulled the lion's teeth, but, for a time, the beast still has some claws. The war is won, but not over until Jesus comes again to complete human history. In the time remaining to the enemy, which grows shorter with each moment, he works his own evangelism program to ensnare humans with temptation and lies. Between Christ's victory over Satan and the end of time, our warfare is akin to a "mop-up" operation, applying the consequences of defeat to a beaten enemy who has not yet stopped fighting. Authority and the truth are our main weapons, and we should wield them daily.

By the cross, the Lord has brought Satan under his authority. That same authority is our heritage because we are sons and daughters of God. Satan roams about behaving as though no one had authority over him. When we fail to exercise our authority as Christians, we allow him to get away with it. Taking authority over the enemy may simply mean commanding him to cease a particular effort he is directing against us or someone for whom we are responsible. Or it may mean taking determined steps to shut out his influence. For example, we may need to avoid places or people who weaken our resistance to Satan's temptations. To fight temptation is to exercise our divinely appointed authority. This perspective adds a pleasant twist to the grueling business of resisting temptation. Taking authority allows us the pleasure of subduing the enemy, instead of being subdued by him.

Chastened by his defeat at the cross and restrained by the hand of God from using more dangerous methods, Satan's main weapons are now lies. As members of the new humanity, we come into a position of authority over him, a fact that stings the pride of this renegade archangel. While he awaits the final, inevitable humbling, his only chance to trick us into joining him is by lying. He lies to us about God's love, our salvation, our personal security in Christ, our sonship. He lies about our spouse's fidelity, our friend's loyalty, our child's obedience. He tempts us to act wrongly and tries to convince us that we have no strength to resist. When Jesus was tempted—and he was really and sorely tried by Satan's lies—he came through the test by repeating simple, confident statements of the truth. Knowing the truth and holding ourselves to it is our best defense against the devil.

Our authority in Jesus and our conviction of God's truth will win the day, every day, for us as we battle the enemy outside the walls. Now we must turn our attention to release from the enemy within. Sin works in us through the collaboration of our flesh. Overcoming the flesh and the problems it causes is mainly the work of the Holy Spirit in us. Our release from this enemy comes when we learn to surrender our lives fully to Christ and yield ourselves to the power of his Holy Spirit. How to go about this is the subject of the remaining chapters.

SIX

The New Captain

IF CHRISTIANS EXPECT their problems to disappear by some magic, they are profoundly mistaken. Becoming a Christian normally means having to deal with more problems rather than less. No one experiences their patterns of sinful behavior as problems until they know they must get rid of them. Becoming alive to the work of the Holy Spirit can bring to light problems that have long been hidden. When clear, fresh water is poured into a soiled bucket, all the dirt is flushed to the surface. The same is true of the Christian's life. But instead of greeting the situation with dismay, Christians should be glad for the chance to clean up the mess.

As we have seen, our problems in the Christian life are rooted in the activities of our foes. The Lord's solution for us was radical. By the work of Christ and the work of the Holy Spirit he has released us from the hold of Satan, the world, sin, and the flesh. Through our commitment to the Lord and our baptism into him, we receive the Holy Spirit. He joins us to the new humanity under the authority and care of Jesus Christ, the

Second Adam. By the power of the Spirit we undergo a fundamental internal change: we have put off the old man with his practices and have put on the new man, who is being renewed in knowledge after the image of his creator (Col 3:9-10).

What the Christian finds in his everyday experience is that, on the one hand, he is a new man being renewed by the Holy Spirit. On the other hand, he discovers, sometimes to his great surprise, that the old man still lurks in the corners. It would not be so bad if the old man would lie there and play dead. But no, not only does he not lie still, he stirs up a little resistance here and he makes a little contact with an outside enemy there. Before long the old man—our flesh—threatens to overwhelm us.

When we recognize this plight, we have a choice. We can either decide what has to change and gather the strength of our will to do it. Or we can decide that this is a problem for the Holy Spirit to handle and turn it over to him. Which of the two would you choose? If you select the first approach, you may as well put down this book. Most Christians have tried it and have demonstrated conclusively that it does not work.

One reason why we sometimes have difficulty surrendering a problem to the power and authority of the Holy Spirit is that we don't understand how to do it very well. We don't have much experience in yielding areas of our life to him. I think the following story will help.

The New Captain and the Old Captain

Imagine that you are employed as an officer on a magnificent ocean liner. Your life aboard ship is very difficult. Not only is the job demanding, but what's worse, the captain is a cruel man. Vile and arrogant, he acts out of caprice rather than reason. His orders always seem completely arbitrary and counterproductive. His regular fits of rage sometimes climax in beatings. Occasionally he adopts an excessively pleasant manner to conceal some nasty plan.

His tyranny over the crew and passengers continues until the owner of the company takes a cruise on the liner. He notices the problems caused by the captain, and he takes action that very day by firing him and putting a new captain in charge. The new captain makes quite a contrast to the old one. He is good and strong, a man everyone respects and obeys. He knows how to lead the crew, to bring things back into order, and to care for all the people on the ship.

But the old captain does not leave the liner, even though the president of the company had directed him to. He takes up residence in a storage room deep in the ship's hold. There, bitterly resenting his ouster, he nurses his ill feelings toward the company and the new captain. Occasionally, he strolls about the ship menacing the crew just as he used to when he was captain. He barks orders that contradict the new captain's directions. Out of fear and a strange forgetfulness, crew members often do what he says.

On one of these strolls, the old captain struts into your office and gives you his orders for the day, just as he used to. When you start to resist, he bullies you with threats. You are now faced with a choice. You could try to handle the situation on your own. You have always wanted to put the old captain down. You are a little bigger than he, and you suspect that you are a whole lot stronger. You would enjoy smashing him one or somehow taking care of the matter yourself. Or you could bring the matter to the attention of the new captain. You could say to the old captain, "You must be making some mistake. I don't work for you any more. Have you forgotten about the new captain. You'll need to take up the matter with him. In fact, here he is right now. Why don't you talk to him about it?" Instead of relying on yourself, you can place the problem under the authority of the new captain, letting him deal with the old captain and his antics.

This parallels our situation as Christians. Through the power of Christ's death and resurrection, we have put off the old man with his evil ways and put on the new man. The old captain has been fired, and we are under the authority of the new captain. When our flesh, behaving like the old captain, attempts to usurp its old place of power in order to mold us according to its ways, we face the same choice as the officer in the story. We have the option of trying to handle our flesh on our own or of turning the matter over to the Lord, letting him deal with our flesh and its bag of tricks.

Many of us find the first option attractive. Our flesh has caused us difficulty for years. Wouldn't it be fun to muscle it into place for once? We think we're a little bit bigger than it is now. But the better and safer option is to place the problem under the authority of our new captain.

Yielding our problems to the Holy Spirit within us requires that we change our approach. We must renounce all possibility of handling things by ourselves. We must stop trying to do the right thing on our own. We should stop demanding that God help us do things *our* way. We must refuse to follow the commands of our flesh. We must rely on the authority of the Lord and the power of the Spirit to resolve our problems. Our new captain has the power to subdue our flesh.

Making Christ the Lord

Accomplishing the switch means turning every area of our lives over to the Lord. In the story, the new captain had to take authority over life on the ocean liner in every detail. One of the first things he did when he assumed his responsibilities was to tour the entire ship, exploring every hold and stateroom, talking to crew and passengers alike. He was both assessing conditions and extending his authority over every area of the ship.

The same thing must happen for us. We must give every area of our lives over to the Lord. Our new captain makes his exploratory tour, assessing conditions and extending his authority throughout our lives. Since everything must come under his lordship, we would be wise to throw open every nook and cranny for his attention.

If we take inventory now, however, we will probably find that we have held back some areas. An honest look at the places where our old captain—the flesh—operates will uncover more work for the Lord. When we have a problem that will not go away, an objective assessment will tell us exactly what it is we have yet to yield to Christ's authority.

Sometimes we even seal off an area, secretly hoping that the Lord will overlook it. Our new captain approaches a closed door and gently inquires, "What's in there?"

Surprised that he even noticed the door, we respond nervously, "Nothing."

"Well," he continues kindly, "if it's nothing, I don't suppose you'll mind if I have a look."

As he moves again towards the door, we quickly step in front of it. "It didn't occur to me that you would ever want to go in *there*," we say.

"Oh, but I do. You're ready for it" is his reply.

"I don't think I want you to see what's there" is our truthful answer.

It is possible for a Christian both to desire to follow the Lord in everything and to attempt to shut him out of an area where we are having a problem. The following account illustrates the point further.

Leo is the owner of a small business and a leader

in a Christian group that evangelizes teenagers. He is very effective at both responsibilities. Leo is twenty-eight, married, with one child, and is an evangelical who has been following the Lord with conviction since he was fifteen years old. But occasionally he would have bouts with depression, though he never regarded it as much of a problem. However, Laura, his wife of three years, thought otherwise. She told Leo that his brief periods of sluggishness and withdrawal were difficult times for her. On those days, Leo, usually a very good husband, would renege on his responsibilities, letting her fend for herself. Because he knew that he was making life difficult for Laura, Leo made some efforts to stop getting depressed. But it was a struggle he could not seem to win. As he prayed about it, he began to realize that he enjoyed getting depressed. That was the root of the problem. He wasn't able to receive the Lord's help because he liked dropping out now and then.

As soon as Leo told the Lord that he did not want to get depressed anymore, he was finally able to overcome his bouts with depression. Instead of giving in to his flesh, which kept repeating its invitations to him to take a little vacation and withdraw, he gave the area over to the Lord. In effect, he said to his flesh, "There must be some mistake. I don't have to obey you any longer. Have you forgotten the new captain? Here he is right now. Why don't you ask him if he'd like to go on a little vacation and withdraw with you?"

Leo had told the Lord: "I want to change; I

don't like the idea of getting depressed. I want you to deal with my flesh and set me free of this impulse." And God worked the change Leo asked for. Yielding to the Lord released him from the hold of the flesh. For the past eight years Leo has had control of the area, knowing he had it within his power to refuse to get depressed. Most of the time, with one or two slips, he has chosen well.

Take another example. Betty is a single woman about forty years old. Like Mark, whom we met in the first chapter, she has had a problem with sexual fantasies. For many years, discipline and willpower helped Betty manage the area somewhat, but she still regarded her sexual daydreaming as a fairly serious problem.

Things got worse a few years ago after she attended a seminar on sexuality for single people. The seminar was a well-intentioned effort to help single Christians confront their sexuality and deal with it more openly. In Betty's case it was a disaster. For a while afterward she indulged her fantasies. She also began to have a problem with masturbation, something that had never been a problem for her before. One of the books recommended at the seminar suggested that single people allow themselves to become secretly infatuated with a member of the opposite sex. Betty tried it and was embarrassed about the crush she developed on a young married man in her church.

That bit of ridiculous advice was a blessing in disguise. Betty was so revolted by her experience that she rejected the book and the seminar. She talked the area over with a married woman who had been her friend for years. This lady suggested to Betty that she had not yet won her struggle with sexual fantasy and masturbation because she had not really turned the area over to the Lord. While she wanted to stop, Betty found her sexual fantasies a little too pleasant. In prayer, Betty told the Lord that she wanted the sexual area to work right for her. She said she wanted to change and asked him to give her the self-control she needed to curb her unruly desires.

Betty does not yet have complete mastery of the area, but she has improved considerably since she began to ask the Lord to change her. Her problem with masturbation seems to be over. She still has times when disorderly sexual thoughts seem to overwhelm her. But she gives in to these thoughts less frequently and is now confident that the Lord will give her greater control in that area as well.

A key to being able to yield a problem to the Lord is simply to *want* to be changed in that area.

So far, we have uncovered three basic steps for overcoming persistent problems in our life. These principles (and others in subsequent chapters) will be the makings of a strategy that will help us to overcome the flesh. The first three parts in the strategy are as follows:

1. We must honestly admit that we have a problem.

2. We must place it under the Lord's authority for him to correct, setting aside our tendency to handle it on our own.

3. We must want to be changed so much that we will examine our life carefully enough to root out whatever it is that we are attached to.

SEVEN

Is Jesus Big Enough?

CHRISTIANS ARE ACQUAINTED with several different kinds of faith. First, there is the kind of faith that is expressed when people make an adult commitment to the Lord. They exercise a certain kind of faith that brings them into a personal relationship with Jesus Christ. This faith makes a connection with God. Through it, they appropriate the basic elements of their relationship with the Lord—baptism, life in the Holy Spirit, membership in the church. This is the kind of faith that makes us Christians.

Second, we also use the word *faith* for the assent we give to the truths of Christianity. When our intellect submits to a truth of scripture, we say we believe it. When we accept the truths declared in the Apostles' Creed—the Trinity, the Incarnation, the Redemption, the Church—we say we believe. This is doctrinal faith and it is the guarantor of Christian orthodoxy.

Christians also have a third kind of faith, an underlying trust in God that can be called daily faith. This faith assures us that the Lord provides and cares for us. God sustains us in being, keeps us from harm, anticipates our needs, knows our thoughts. We know these to be facts and we count on them. This is the faith we live by.

These varieties of faith are all good and useful. In fact, they are essential. But they are distinct from the kind of faith we need to overcome problems rooted in the flesh. We can possess all three and yet not be able to conquer a persistent difficulty in our life.

John, for example, was a Lutheran in good standing at his church. From the day of his profession and confirmation of faith as a teenager, he had won the admiration of the entire congregation. An excellent college student, he was a youth leader in the church and taught Sunday school to thirteen-year-old boys. If there were a way to test the kinds of faith present in a person, John would rate high on all three varieties described above.

John's father had abandoned his family when John was twelve. Consequently, John had a rough time of it in the next few years. As a teenager, he developed a number of emotional problems, which he took with him into adulthood, though he kept them hidden from others. He had to deal constantly with guilt feelings that had accumulated to mountain-high proportions. Beneath those feelings of guilt, he felt a profound self-hatred. Underneath the surface of his articulate self-confidence, John was often troubled by self-contempt. When he exercised leadership at church, he often thought of himself as a hypocrite.

One day, as John was talking over his problems with a family friend he had grown to trust, the man exclaimed, "John, you think your problem is so big—you're so proud of your sins—that you think Jesus himself isn't big enough to help you." The man continued to say that though John believed in the Lord, he didn't really expect the Lord to do anything about his problems. In fact, John did not believe that the Lord *could* do anything about them.

Expectant Faith

John wasn't able to overcome his self-hatred because he failed to exercise the right kind of faith. Overcoming problems rooted in the flesh requires *expectant* faith. Expectant faith believes the Lord will do what must be done to set us free. This is the kind of faith David exercised in his combat with Goliath. Even as he released the polished stone from his sling, he fully expected that it would strike Goliath's unprotected forehead. He knew the Lord would act to save him.

When the apostles urged the Lord, saying, "Increase our faith!" Jesus responded: "If you had faith the size of a mustard seed, you could say to this sycamore, 'Be uprooted and transplanted into the sea, and it would obey you'" (Lk 17:5-6). Jesus was teaching them about expectant faith.

Once, on the road to Jerusalem, Jesus cursed a fig tree that bore no fruit, and it withered on the spot. The disciples asked why this happened.

Jesus said in reply, "Truly, I say to you, if you have faith and never doubt, you will not only do what has been done to the fig tree, but even if you say to this mountain, 'Be taken up and cast into the sea,' it will be done. And whatever you ask in prayer, you will receive, if you have faith" (Mt 21:21-22). Expectant faith begins to look for the desired change the moment the prayer is spoken.

Our problems may seem bigger than the mountain that the Lord pointed to, promising that faith could cast it into the sea. They may be more deeply entrenched than the sycamore tree that faith could pluck out of the ground like a carrot. In order to experience release from them, however, we must be confident that God will act to deliver us. And why shouldn't we be confident? The very same Holy Spirit that raised Jesus Christ from the dead is at work in us (Rom 8:11). Isn't the Lord big enough to free us from our problems? You would think that as Christians, men and women who know and love the Lord, we would have no difficulty believing that Jesus has the power to deal with anything we come up against. After all, we have seen him prevail in valiant combat with Satan.

In *The Great Divorce* C.S. Lewis describes what the outskirts of heaven might be like. In that region, one butterfly could devour all hell with one small bite, if the Lord so allowed. That is reality. Of course Jesus is big enough to overcome all of our problems, and even delicate creatures dwelling in the foothills of his kingdom can chew up hell itself and spit out the bones.

Yet we lose sight of this fact in everyday Christian life. Our problems loom up to shadowy heights, and Jesus seems dwarfed as we grope among these giants. When we read in scripture things like "Whatever you ask in my name, I will do it" (Jn 14:13-14), we say, "Yes, of course that's true." But in our mind's eye we add a little footnote to the text that says, "except for me; I'm different."

Holding Ourselves to the Truth

When we think this way we are being double-minded, a malady that weakens our faith. James diagnoses our condition thus: "But let him ask in faith, with no doubting, for he who doubts is like a wave of the sea that is driven and tossed by the wind. For that person must not suppose that a double-minded man, unstable in all his ways, will receive anything from the Lord" (Jas 1:6-8). The double-minded person opens a chasm between the truth and his problem. The truth is that Jesus is bigger than our problems. With a double mind we say, "Yes, I believe that, but I really don't think I'll ever overcome this problem." The chasm is right there between the *yes* and the *but*. Only expectant faith can bridge that gap. When we exercise that kind of faith we not only know the truth, we hold ourselves to it.

In his letter to the Romans, Paul acknowledges that they *know* they are no longer bound to commit sin. They have truly participated in the death of Christ. But he reminds them that it's not enough to simply know the truth; they must *hold themselves to it*: "So you also must consider yourselves dead to sin and alive to God in Christ Jesus" (Rom 6:11). If we know a fact but fail to hold ourselves to it, we may contradict it by our actions. If I know that I have three thousand dollars but act as though I haven't a cent to my name, I may soon find myself starving. The same is true for the life of faith.

If the power of the Holy Spirit which courses through my life is to strengthen and free me from the effects of the flesh, I must act according to my knowledge of God's presence and power. Expectant faith need not be some majestic bridge over the chasm between knowing the truth and holding myself to it. My faith need only be a tiny key, mustard-seed-size, to unlock the channels of divine power that Jesus has already put at my disposal. Expectant faith holds me to the fact that Jesus is bigger than my problems, and he will unleash storms of his grace to conquer them.

Very often we fail to exercise expectant faith for our problems. We have tried almost everything and have had little or no success. Our discouragement over a particular problem has matured into despair. It has settled securely around the problem area and turned to stone. We can't budge it. We have lost all hope of getting free of it.

We know that something of this order has

happened to us when we find ourselves saying, "Well, that's just the way I am. We are all going to have to live with it." (Someone might justifiably respond, "What do you mean *we*? Maybe you have decided to live with it, friend, but that doesn't mean I have.")

As we take stock of our lives, we may very well find one or two problems that resist change, no matter how much faith we muster. These are areas in which we may have to fight for the faith to see them corrected. In Tolkien's *The Lord of the Rings*, Gandalf faces off against a mighty, evil creature, a Balrog, on the bridge at Khazad Dum. The wizard declares the truth to the Balrog, that by virtue of the authority bestowed on Gandalf it cannot pass. Gandalf destroys the bridge, casting the flaming beast into the pit, but with a whisk of its tail, the Balrog drags the wizard with him. Gandalf is locked in conflict with this fiery beast in the bowels of the earth. He endures the white heat of the fire and is dragged up endless stairs to a mountaintop where he finally conquers this servant of the enemy. He had to fight for faith. He was a steward of the affairs of Middle Earth, charged with its defense against the gathering storm. Yet darkness had reached out to claim him. He hung on and fought until, at the last moment, an eagle rescued him from death itself.

Christians facing difficult problems must imitate this brand of "fight." Doggedness is a common companion to expectant faith. Nothing should daunt us, be it temptation, fire, darkness, or height. If we are tempted to give in, we must fight to hold on to faith. If Gandalf seems too far removed from reality, take the Lord himself for your model. The Lord expected his Father to restore him to life. Jesus attained the glory of the resurrection only by fighting through his crucifixion and death. He had to fight for faith, even though he knew the Father's plan. You may try to dismiss this by saying that Jesus was God, but he was also a man, one like us, who had weaknesses, fears, and doubts (Heb 4:14-15, 5:7-8). In the face of death, the man Jesus fought for faith. He won his battle in the garden on the eve of his death. His winning makes our fighting easier and our victory assured.

Contrary to the way it might seem at first, fighting for faith is not a lapse into willpower Christianity. By definition, willpower Christianity leaves faith out. It works not by faith, but by self-reliance. Fighting for faith is the alternative, both to giving up on the problem and to making one last attempt to handle it ourselves. Fighting through will keep us in touch with the only power that can save us.

It was fifteen years ago that John, the young Lutheran, began to believe that Jesus Christ was bigger than his self-contempt. Now, as a result of expecting the Lord to change him, his problem with self-hatred is only a memory. If he has any problem in that area now it may be one of overconfidence. Jesus is big enough. Are we ready to expect him to release us from our problems?

We can now add the fourth step to our strategy for overcoming the flesh:

> We must expect the Lord to change us. It is not enough to know that Jesus is bigger than our problems; we must hold ourselves to that truth, even to the point of fighting to lay hold of it.

EIGHT

In All Things, God Works

Taking stock of our problems has its drawbacks. As we compute the number of things that are wrong in our lives, we may be staggered by the sum. Reading books (like this one) that offer to help us overcome our problems may even increase our difficulties before they bring relief. We may learn, for example, that some qualities we regarded as virtues are actually vices. We may discover that areas we never paid much attention to are actually traps from which we should get free. In short, the effect of tallying up our problems may only be to put our focus on the problem themselves.

At times, one or another of our more persistent problems may stir up so much turmoil that we can think of almost nothing else. Anxiety and suppressed anger can so agitate us that they absorb all of our mental energy. We may become so preoccupied with some personality defect that we spend all our time worrying about how to change. We might even locate the nexus of all our problems in some act of habitual wrongdoing, such as drunkenness, and become determined to quit. Nothing is wrong with trying to get free of our problems. But taking stock of our problems can fix our eyes on ourselves to a degree that is spiritually unhealthy.

Self-concern prevents us from getting free of the very problems that generate it. Putting our attention on the problems disconnects us from the power of the Holy Spirit, our only real hope for release from their grip.

In All Circumstances

But how, in practical terms, can we turn away from our problems and turn toward the Lord for help? The most effective approach is based on the New Testament principle of rejoicing and giving thanks to the Lord in all circumstances. "Rejoice always, pray constantly, give thanks in all circumstances" (1 Thes 5:16-18). Joy and thankfulness are not unpredictable emotions but qualities that underlie the Christian life. We should be joyful and thankful not only in good times, when we feel happy or grateful, but in bad times as well.

In the culture of the New Testament, to rejoice meant primarily to engage in the activities of celebration: singing, dancing, feasting, and so on. One could rejoice whether he felt happy or not. It is possible that some of those neighbors dragged in to rejoice with the woman who found the dime she had lost might not have felt like partying that day. The point is plain. We can rejoice even in painful circumstances without having to feel happy about them. The command is to be joyful *always*. We are to give thanks in *all* circumstances. According to Paul, thankfulness is the proper response to every circumstance, both good and bad. He didn't say, "Rejoice sometimes, pray occasionally, give thanks in most circumstances."

To rejoice and give thanks in the midst of our problems is not to say that these problems are good. Problems are not good, but evil. We have every reason for wanting to be free of them. Why then does the New Testament teach us to rejoice in the face of difficulties? Though our difficulties are not good in themselves, they can lead to something good. "Count it all joy, my brethren," counsels James, "when you meet various trials, for you know that the testing of your faith produces steadfastness. And let steadfastness have its full effect, that you may be perfect and complete, lacking in nothing" (Jas 1:2-4). We are to be glad for trials because every time we pass through them, we will become more like our Father, who is perfect and complete.

The New Testament teaches us to approach our problems in a way that maintains our connection to the power of God. "We know that in everything God works for good with those who love him, who are called according to his purpose" (Rom 8:28). We have all heard this passage paraphrased as "all things work for good." But the phrase "all things work for good" misplaces the emphasis. Paul actually says, "in everything *God works*." In good and bad, virtue and vice, righteousness and wrongdoing—God works. It is not that we should sin in order to see grace abound. Rather, our problems are reasons for rejoicing and giving thanks because they are opportunities for us to see the power of God at work in our lives.

Once we grasp this truth, we must act on it. When we are suffering from a problem, we must thank the Lord for working it to our good. But be forewarned. We will hardly ever feel like thanking God during these times. Fortunately, the New Testament doesn't require us to feel good about our trials and difficulties but to rejoice in the good that the Lord will work through them. We too readily equate rejoicing with feeling happy, which, though related, are not identical. Most of our problems involve a certain amount of mental or physical pain. In the midst of our anguish, we should thank God for the chance to see him at work. We should express our eagerness to behold the change he will accomplish in us as a consequence.

The following account illustrates how this principle works. Tony is a member of the personnel department in a computer software company. He and his wife, Jean, have five children under ten years of age, a fact related to his problem. He and Jean are both faithful Roman Catholics. After the birth of their fourth child, they began using various methods of natural family planning.

When Jean became pregnant with child number five, both were very surprised, to put it mildly. Motherly instincts soon softened Jean's fears and her sense of inadequacy. She was delighted with the thought of a new baby but knew that Tony wasn't at all happy about it.

Tony has never been known for controlling his temper. His Christian behavior has occasionally been marred by angry outbursts or by quiet, but intense, periods of slow burn. The surprise pregnancy put him in a state that ran the entire gamut of anger's possibilities. At first he was livid. Even though he stopped having outbursts, his rage simmered within and became mixed with a deep discouragement. For a month he was profoundly out-of-sorts, a condition that contributed to other problems. For example, he misinterpreted the behavior of his supervisor at work, complaining bitterly and unfairly about his boss to Jean and others. His constant, suppressed fury drained and exhausted him.

When Tony's anger showed no signs of going away, his close friend Joe confronted him about it. For several years it had been Tony and Joe's habit to meet for lunch once a week to talk about their lives and to pray for their families. When the bout of temper struck, Tony started missing the lunch dates. Joe cornered him and the two friends spent several hours talking. After hearing Tony out, Joe advised him to thank the Lord every time discouragement or anger smoldered in his heart. "That's easy for you to say," snarled Tony. "Your wife isn't pregnant." But after he had thought about Joe's words and recognized the wisdom in them, Tony began to follow his advice.

For the next month, many times each day, Tony simply thanked the Lord. At first he did it with great difficulty. It didn't seem to make a difference; he still felt miserable, angry, and discouraged. "I'm very angry, Lord," he would say, "but I'm grateful to you for all that you are doing in me. Please help Jean, for I think I'm causing her a lot of pain." It wasn't long before the thanksgiving came more easily. Before the month was over his anger had subsided. He repented to Jean for his bad behavior. Soon Tony himself began to look forward to the birth of the baby.

Tony says that ever since then he as handled his anger more effectively. He still has to be wary, but he has more control. Expressing thankfulness in the face of a problem opens a channel for the Lord's power to flow where it would otherwise remain blocked by self-concern. If we remain focused on the problem, we are stuck and may get hurt. The moment we turn our minds actively to the Lord, we place ourselves in a position to receive God's help and to be strengthened in the process.

Accepting Crosses

Sometimes, people deal with problems by accepting them as crosses. This may be precisely the approach the Lord wants us to take. If so, an attitude of rejoicing and thanksgiving won't make the problem go away, but it will give us the right disposition towards God.

If we become convinced that a certain difficulty is a cross we should accept, we need to have the correct perspective about it. A person who accepts a problem as a cross ought to be clear about its source. Crosses do *not* come from the Lord. Paul was afflicted by some personal suffering which no one has been able to identify. He speaks about it only once: "A thorn was given me in the flesh, a messenger of Satan to harass me, to keep me from being too elated" (2 Cor 12:7). He may allow us to undergo some trial, but Satan is the one who originated the trial. With this perspective, a cross does not become something we are proud of or a badge we grow attached to. It remains an implement of the devil, a "messenger of Satan," useful to God in disciplining us. If and when the job is done, we should gladly set aside any particular cross we have been carrying.

Furthermore, we shouldn't think that crosses in themselves are good. The cross of Christ was purely evil, the nexus of all that is sinful and opposed to God. Satan used it to try to obliterate the Lord. If we accept some problem as a cross, we should understand that the problem is not itself something good. At the same time, we know that the Father brought unfathomable good from the cross of his Son and wills to bring good out of our suffering. Accepting something as a cross, then, means acknowledging that a problem is an evil through which the Lord is working for our benefit. It is another opportunity for grace to conquer the hold of the flesh on us.

Joy and thanks in all circumstances is the fifth part of our strategy for getting free from persistent problems. We can state it thus:

We must express joy and thanks to the Lord in our problems. Joy and thankfulness transform our problems into opportunities for the Lord to work in our lives. They turn our minds from our problems to him.

Tearing Up the IOUs

A YOUNG FRENCH SCHOOLBOY watched as two Englishmen disembarked from their ship at the port of Calais. Before they knew what hit them, the lad charged at them, pushing them off the pier into the water. Not too pleased at this inhospitable gesture, the men climbed out and accosted the boy. "Just what are you trying to do? Is that any way to greet visitors to your country? A good spanking might teach you some manners. Why did you do such a thing?"

The boy spat back, "That's for burning Joan of Arc at the stake!"

"But that happened five hundred years ago," was the astonished response.

"Yea, but I just learned about it this morning," came the reply.

Nationality jokes are banned at my house (I am not allowed to tell them). However, as instruction in a certain dangerous human weakness, such humor does have redeeming value. Like the boy in the anecdote, people tend to hold grudges against one another for a long time. Nations may nurse bitter memories of past rivalries for centuries;

individuals may do it for years. In any case, resentment is an unhealthy practice and detrimental to all involved.

Nursing grudges is a serious stumbling block in the Christian life. Constantly recalling someone's offense and thinking of ways to pay them back creates a steady drain on our spiritual energy. Bitterness prevents us from receiving the Lord's power. It blocks our release from the problems that afflict us.

Resentment has a boomerang effect. Only rarely do we succeed in damaging an offender more than we damage ourselves. The harder we try to get back at someone, the more we get hurt. As our mind reaches out in search of revenge, bitterness reaches in to us, plunging it's massive, expanding tentacle deep within us. Daydreams of getting even devour our time during the day. At night we lose sleep to our hurt feelings. Resentment is a spiritual tapeworm that nourishes itself at our expense. Too often we are willing to feed this parasite.

Revenge can seem so reasonable. It doesn't take much to persuade us that we have good cause to strike back. Four-year-old Mary runs in tears to her father with the complaint, "Daddy, Daddy, Tommy hit me for no reason." The wise father responds, "Tell him he had better have a reason." Five-year-old Tommy is next on the scene, explaining to his dad that the reason he hit Mary was that she hit him first. Like the children in this all too familiar scene, we often have good reasons for striking back at the way people have treated us.

Many times we are perfectly right. In accordance with principles of strict justice, people who wrong us ought to repent and make amends for the damage they have done.

A Standard of Mercy

While this approach makes sense on one level, it can be fatal to us on another. If it is reasonable to hold others to a standard of strict justice, it is equally reasonable to hold ourselves to the same standard. Had the Lord demanded payment for the debt we piled up because of our sins, it would have cost each of us our lives. Death would have been only fair punishment for us. What else could we expect?

The Lord, however, dealt with us according to a different standard, a standard of mercy. He was not put off by our sin. In the face of an endless inventory of wrongdoing—direct offenses against his Person—he sent his Son to an ignominious death to cancel our debt to him. "While we were still weak, at the right time Christ died for the ungodly. Why, one will hardly die for a righteous man—though perhaps for a good man one will dare even to die. But God shows his love for us in that while we were yet sinners Christ died for us" (Rom 5:6-8). Instead of exacting what we owed him, the Lord forgave us. Paul says that the Lord "canceled the bond which stood against us with its legal demands; this he set aside, nailing it to the cross" (Col 2:14).

If we want the Lord to release us from our

wrongdoing, we must release others from the wrongs they have done to us. This is what we pray in the Lord's Prayer. Instructed by Jesus himself, we ask the Father to bestow the same measure of forgiveness on us as we bestow on others. If we have been stingy with our forgiveness up until now, we had best hasten to become more generous. We ought to understand the consequences of praying the Lord's Prayer. We do not want to commit ourselves to a niggardly measure of forgiveness and mercy each time we say, "And forgive us our trespasses *as* we forgive those who trespass against us."

If we are harboring resentment, grudges, or bitterness against others, the New Testament commands us to put them away. "Let all bitterness and wrath and anger and clamor and slander be put away from you, with all malice, and be kind to one another, tenderhearted, forgiving one another, as God in Christ forgave you" (Eph 4:31).

When we hold a grudge against someone, we are holding a claim against them. We write out spiritual IOUs. We keep strict accounts, planning to exact the very last penny. In our ledger, we hold IOUs against our parents (for quarreling between themselves and manipulating us); against brothers and sisters (for belittling us and getting more parental attention, or so it seemed); against spouses (for some petty fault or slip of the tongue); against children (for lack of respect and for turning out different than we planned). We hold IOUs against friends, neighbors, co-workers, acquaintances, and so on. If we are to experience freedom ourselves, we must cancel all these debts. We must deal with our IOUs the way God dealt with his (Col 2:14).

Getting Rid of Resentment

There is a practical way to get rid of resentment. Make a list of all those people toward whom you have resentments. Begin with the people closest to you—parents, spouses, brothers, sisters, and children—and move outwards from there. You might want to list each on a separate slip of paper, and then tear up the IOUs one by one. Forgive each of them, no matter what they have done to offend you.

You may come up against one or two IOUs that you feel you just can't tear up, because the hurt was too big. Consider this situation. Sally is the eldest of four daughters. Her father divorced her mother after twenty-five years of an unhappy marriage. With good reason, all their daughters have sided with their mother. Sally alone has forgiven her father. The others resent him bitterly and their own lives are beginning to show telltale signs of this root of bitterness. Each of them has asked for Sally's advice since they know she is at peace over the matter. When Sally tells her sisters to forgive their father, each says, "I can't bring myself to do that. What *else* can I do, Sally? Please help me." There is nothing these young women can do until they forgive their father. Their resentment is a block that cannot be ignored.

Sally's sisters are making a common mistake. They think that forgiveness is something a person *feels* rather than something a person *does*. If Sally's sisters wait until they feel like forgiving their father, they will probably take his IOU with them to the grave. It helps to feel like forgiving someone we must forgive, but if we don't, we should go ahead and forgive them anyway. Once we have torn up the IOUs, our feelings toward the person will improve. Through the power of forgiveness, many a person has ended up liking someone they thought they would always hate.

Tearing up IOUs is usually a unilateral action. For our part we release people who have offended us. We say by our action that we no longer intend to collect whatever it is we think they owe us. Tearing up IOUs does not mean going to each person toward whom we feel resentful and saying, "I forgive you for the time you did this" or "I don't hold that against you anymore." Usually putting aside resentments and bitterness is something I do privately, between me and the Lord. However, the process can suggest ways of straightening out broken relationships. We should be open to taking further steps if they seem right. Talking over what we think we must do with a person we trust may spare us from making a serious mistake.

The Lord gives us the grace to forgive and forgive generously. We should begin now by tearing up the IOUs we are holding, and we should repeat the process regularly.

We can now add a sixth part to our strategy for getting free from the influence of the flesh:

> We must put aside all resentment, bitterness, and grudges. These are obstacles to our spiritual freedom which prevent us from experiencing the power of the Lord in our lives.

TEN

The Battle for Our Minds

THERE IS AN OLD SAYING that goes something like this: "Though many birds may fly around your head, you don't have to let them nest in your hair." There's a kernel of wisdom to this saying, which we would do well to take seriously. Innumerable thoughts pass through our minds every day, each one clamoring for attention and looking for a place to settle in. If we welcome them all, we'll be in trouble. We must be very selective about those we choose to make our own.

Our thoughts significantly influence our actions. It is a mistake to believe that even passing thoughts have no effect on us. That is simply not true. As a human being, we are an integrated whole, not a collection of independent units. What we see and touch affects our thinking. What we think and imagine affects our behavior.

If we are to make any progress in overcoming the flesh, we must take a concern for our minds. Remember, the flesh works in our intellect. That may even be the main way it works in our lives. Jesus said that evil thoughts corrupt us. "But what comes out of the mouth proceeds from the heart, and this defiles a man. For out of the heart come evil thoughts, murder, adultery, fornication, theft, false witness, slander" (Mt 15:18-19). Wrongdoing does not just "happen"; it is the fruit of wicked contemplation.

When we put on the new man and put off the old, we are given a new mind. Paul says, "Be renewed in the spirit of your minds, and put on the new nature [the new man], created after the likeness of God in true righteousness and holiness" (Eph 4:23). The new man has the mind of Christ, a mind that directs us in good behavior. But the old man, you will recall, does not slink off and disappear as he ought. He lingers, putting his thoughts into our heads. The mind of the new man works like a finely tuned gyroscope, governing our behavior from within, under the influence of the Holy Spirit. But the mind of the old man operates like radar, locating the attractive, but dangerous, influences of the world system outside.

Since more voices than just our own speak in our thoughts, we should not automatically assume that what we think is what we are. We are not responsible for every thought that flits through our minds. The flesh is behind some of them, and we can be sure it is not trying to influence us for the good.

The Truth about Temptation

A major way that the flesh attacks our minds is by planting temptations in it. Not a few ordinary men and women, for example, barraged by homosexual temptations, hear a persistent voice that says, "You're a homosexual. You won't be happy until you face up to it and accept it." That is the old man speaking. His radar won't have to sweep very far afield in our progressive Western world to find persuasive, corroborative voices that will "help" that man or woman "come out" as a gay. But *these temptations do not say anything factual about the person tempted.* If a person fends off homosexual temptations every day of his life for sixty-five years, those temptations did not make him a homosexual. Temptations do not tell us much, if anything, about the person receiving them. They tell us more about the one sending them. They only reveal the strategy the enemy has chosen to ensnare this son or daughter of God. They expose the enemy's nature rather than any reality about his prey.

We tend to think that temptation is sin, or at least so close to being sin that it is not worth the effort to resist it. Now, if that thought does not come from the flesh, it comes from the devil himself. A temptation that passes through our minds is no different in itself from any other thought. We can decide how we are going to interpret it and whether we are going to embrace it or not. Temptations are only dangerous if we let them take root in our mind. If we keep our distance from them and replace them with other, nobler thoughts, we have dealt with them correctly.

The flesh works on our minds in numerous other ways. It lies to us, deceiving us into thinking that we must sin. The flesh persuades us that we will never be free from this or that problem. The old man brings his cronies home with him, giving them the run of our minds, as though he, and not the Lord, owned the place. At his invitation, discouragement comes in and works us over. Then his companion, despair, takes his turn whipping us.

The flesh supplies a spiritual calculator to help us measure our thoughts and actions according to the standards of our friends and of the seers of Western culture. Our flesh also attempts to define our self-image for us: it would have us believe that we are merely worthless, guilty humans, doomed to be fodder for Satan. If it can get us to feel bad about ourselves, we are easier to push around.

The Proper Care and Feeding of Our Minds

What goes on in our minds, then, has a lot to do with the degree of Christian freedom we experience. Dwelling upon evil thoughts constricts our freedom. Yielding our minds to the Holy Spirit expands it. "For those who live according to the flesh set their minds on the things of the flesh, but those who live according to the Spirit set their minds on the things of the Spirit. To set the mind on the flesh is death, but to set the mind on the Spirit is life and peace. For the mind that is set on the flesh is hostile to God; it does not submit to God's law; indeed it cannot; and those who are in the flesh cannot please God" (Rom 8:5-8). Who do we want to win the battle for our mind, the flesh or the Holy Spirit? If we want the Holy Spirit to prevail, we will need to take an active, rather than a passive, approach. Unless we actively present our minds to the Lord, we will allow our thoughts to welcome among them the voices of evil spirits. Taking active concern for our minds involves both refusing the influence of the flesh and yielding to the grace of the Spirit.

We should regard our minds as a battleground over which the Lord has already prevailed. Now we need only guard the battleground to prevent the old man from moving his troops back into position. The Lord has captured the territory and commissioned us as his lieutenants to hold it in his name. But the enemy would desperately like to reclaim it. Our strategy should be to use the Lord's authority, backed up by his power, to marshal our thoughts. We are fully equipped to keep the flesh from dictating our thoughts and from infiltrating our minds with ideas that come from the enemy. Our job is to refuse to give evil thoughts any place in our minds. We must be diligent about rejecting invitations to sin. We must distance our minds from the parade of negative thoughts competing for attention.

Computer programmers have an expression that applies to our minds as well, "garbage in, garbage out." If the computer generates a jumble of confused material, we can be sure that the source of the problem can be located in what was put into the computer. The same is true for our minds. If they produce evil thoughts that culminate in wicked behavior, we can be sure that one source of the problem has to do with what was put into it. Garbage in, garbage out. Taking an active concern to protect our minds means being wary about what we take in. A cursory review of the media demonstrates that it is increasingly anti-Christian in content. Sensible Christians will not pretend that they can view or read just anything without adverse effects. We must control our reading and viewing carefully.

The action we take to protect our minds is not merely the negative action of refusing evil thoughts. We must also yield our minds to the Holy Spirit. When we put on the new man, we put on the mind of Christ. Paul says that our new man "is being renewed in knowledge after the image of its creator" (Col 3:10). The Holy Spirit activates the mind of Christ in us. He helps us understand the Lord's ways. He confers the practical wisdom we need to apply the teaching of scripture in our daily lives. The Holy Spirit empowers us to resist the evil thoughts of the old man. He implants in us thoughts that bear fruit in righteous behavior.

Yielding our minds to the Holy Spirit means submitting them to the Lord's authority. Paul says that the mind set on the flesh does not, and cannot, submit to God's law. Conversely, the mind set on the Spirit is a mind that submits itself to God's law. Living by the Spirit means believing without question what the Lord says and then obeying him.

If we want the Holy Spirit to inspire and form our thoughts, we must give him something to work with. We are not supposed to still our minds to the point of blankness. Scripture does not tell us to eliminate all thought in order to passively await some distant voice, but rather to fill our minds with good and true thoughts. "Whatever is true, whatever is honorable, whatever is just, whatever is pure, whatever is lovely, whatever is gracious, if there is any excellence, if there is anything worthy of praise, think about these things" (Phil 4:8).

Practically speaking, all of us should read scripture daily, setting aside at least fifteen minutes to fill our minds with inspired thoughts. We should also read sound Christian books and make use of other Christian media. If we fill our minds with excellent materials, we can expect them to produce excellent thoughts that lead to holiness. Taking an active approach to protect our minds is the seventh part of our strategy to attain Christian freedom.

We must guard our thoughts, refusing to let the flesh influence our minds, and yielding our minds instead to the Holy Spirit.

ELEVEN

The Inner Healing
of Relationships

THE NINETEENTH-CENTURY SOCIALISTS believed that the human environment was the source of the evil that human beings experienced. They alleged that economic, social, and political laws generated problems for people. Karl Marx, for example, believed that class struggle was an economic law that chained humanity in misery. Early socialists held that the way to eliminate the influence of evil on man, the way to resolve human problems, was to place humans in the right environment.

Some of them constructed model human communities designed either for agrarian or industrial settings. In controlled situations, where liberty, equality, and fraternity were to operate untrammelled by greed and other wickedness, human beings would excel and prosper. So they reasoned. Planned communities, with carefully designed buildings and grounds and craftily conceived approaches to relationships, work, and survival were attempted in England and America. For the most part, these planned human environments were dismal failures. People didn't behave any better in them than they did in other environments.

Nineteenth-century socialist theory was built on a certain naivete about the human condition. Socialists simply did not believe that human beings were innately flawed. If one removed them from ordinary society in which economic laws, for example, played havoc with them, and placed them in an ideal, planned community, people were supposed to progress to perfection.

This view did not adequately reckon with what humans are up against. These social engineers were like people who would construct a beautifully designed wooden platform over the mouth of an active volcano. What kind of security could such a platform provide? These social engineers did not reckon with the world, sin, or the devil. Many early socialists, in fact, were materialists who scoffed at the idea of any kind of spiritual world, let alone the existence of personal evil spirits.

The fatal weakness of their schemes was that they failed to acknowledge that man is flawed. Human beings are good, but they have evil tendencies that come from the flesh. When people are placed in a carefully planned social environment, they may behave in a good way *or* a bad way. The environment may have an effect on them, but it is not the only thing that determines their behavior. The ordinary social environment is evil because some factors are at work in it to cause problems bigger than the individuals can control.

The work of the flesh in us only contributes to those problems. But moving to a planned community does not deal with the real source of the problems.

A Community of Faith

For all this, there is a kernel of truth in the idea of building healthy human environments. This is precisely what the Lord intended the new humanity to be. Through the work of Christ and the work of the Holy Spirit, the Lord released mankind from the grip of its ancient enemies. Jesus, the second Adam, founded a new race of men and women. They were to live their lives fully for God and in union with one another. This new humanity is the church, and its life is to be lived out in Christian community.

In modern society, Christian community isn't something that just happens. Christians must build it in the midst of ordinary society. For that to happen individuals must be brought to an adult commitment to the Lord and into committed relationships with one another. Not all churches or Christian groups are Christian communities in this sense. Of course, all are part of the Christian community which is the entire new humanity, but local Christian community is something we must work at: developing committed relationships; learning how to care for one another; growing in the freedom to share our whole life with others. None of these come naturally. The flesh does its best to confound our efforts to attain the important elements of community life.

Christians who live in churches, groups, or communities that have built an environment of committed personal relationships seem to have an easier time overcoming the flesh. For many, some kinds of problems seem to go away as a result of living in a Christian environment. Other problems are resolved more slowly but become easier to deal with and correct. Why should committed Christian personal relationships have so great an effect on us? Precisely because many of our personal problems are rooted in twisted personal relationships. Membership in a group or church that has sound relationships can provide the impetus that frees a person from problems that originated in wrong ways of relating. Consider the following examples:

—Jim was a man riddled with fear; it controlled him to the point that he had become emotionally disturbed. He would, at times, be so immobilized by anxiety that he would skip work for a week, isolating himself in his room. Jim tried every conceivable spiritual device to free himself but found no help until he joined a community church. Jim and his pastor attribute his freedom from fear to the fact that he has lived for the last five years in daily contact with men and women who love and serve him.

—Kathy, who had a problem with suppressed anger and shyness, discovered that she changed significantly when she became associated with a small Bible study evangelism group. After seven years with that group, she no longer has a problem with suppressed anger. She has overcome shyness enough to be an effective discussion leader. Kathy recognizes that the foundation for her problem with anger and shyness was built by a long history of bad relationships with her family and friends. Her anger stemmed from her frustration at not being able to deal with the negativity and criticalness that characterized her daily contacts. Shyness protected her from these difficulties. Simple, straightforward relating in the Christian group removed the root of her frustration. The encouragement of others has been a major factor for healing her shyness.

—John, the young Lutheran we met earlier, who began to get free of self-hatred when he decided Jesus was big enough, says that participating faithfully in a prayer group was an important part of his healing. In particular, regular work alongside other Christian men and women who respected him and expressed affection for him made a big difference for his self-image.

Sound Christian relationships can free us from the flesh because they orient us toward the Lord and toward serving others. "Do nothing from selfishness or conceit," Paul instructed the Philippians, "but in humility count others better than yourselves. Let each of you look not only to his own interests, but also to the interests of others" (Phil 2:3-4). Selfishness and conceit are problems that stem from the flesh. Paul's antidote for both is to occupy oneself totally in serving others. But the flesh wants us to keep our eyes on ourselves; it encourages us to focus on our problems. Deliverance from selfishness, conceit, and other problems comes when we take our eyes off ourselves and our problems and begin to meet the needs of others. Once our inward stare is broken, we can more freely turn to the Lord, the only one who can release us from our difficulties.

Inner Healing and Deliverance

Our relationships with other Christian men and women can also provide a context within which we can receive special prayer for release from our problems. This kind of prayer is sometimes called prayer for inner healing and deliverance. It works best in a Christian environment of committed personal relationships, but it is only one of the many approaches that must work together to free us. Relationships and service may be even more important for Christian freedom than a special time of prayer.

Prayer for inner healing and deliverance from the influence of evil spirits uniquely channel the power of God directly into the problem area. We ask the Holy Spirit to release us so that we can take whatever steps we must to receive our freedom. After this time of prayer, we appropriate God's blessings by resolving daily to shake off the influence of the flesh and learn new ways of behaving. The fruit of true inner healing and deliverance is found in a person's daily life. They should be living a more effective Christian life.

Now we can fit the last part of the strategy into place. Committed Christian personal relationships are in themselves an important source of freedom from the grip of the flesh. They turn us to the Lord and to others, providing opportunities for us to appropriate the freedom we have already received through inner healing and deliverance from evil spirits.

Our Strategy

This yields the final practical steps: We must seek the committed Christian personal relationships that are a source of freedom, and we must be open to special prayer for inner healing and deliverance from evil spirits. We have developed a practical strategy for overcoming the grip of the flesh in our lives. Now we can gather together all the parts in order to get a view of the whole approach:

1. We must honestly admit that we have a problem.

2. We must place our problem under the Lord's authority for him to correct, setting aside our tendency to try to handle it on our own.

3. We must want to be changed so much that we will examine the area carefully enough to root out whatever it is that we are attached to.

4. We must expect the Lord to change us. It is not enough to know that Jesus is bigger than our problems; we must hold ourselves to that truth, even to the point of fighting to lay hold of it.

5. We must express joy and thanks to the Lord in our problems. Joy and thanksgiving transform our problems into opportunities for the Lord to work in our lives. They turn our minds from our problems to him.

6. We must put aside all resentment, bitterness, and grudges. These are obstacles to our spiritual freedom which prevent us from experiencing the power of the Lord in our lives.

7. We must guard our thoughts, refusing to let the flesh influence our minds, and yielding our minds instead to the Holy Spirit.

8. We must seek out committed Christian personal relationships which are a source of freedom from the grip of the flesh.

9. We must be open to special prayer for inner healing and deliverance from evil spirits.

There is some risk in setting forth the strategy in this form. It tempts us to begin with a set of rules instead of with the Holy Spirit. If this set of principles subtly seduces us into taking a willpower approach, we will have fallen victim to the old man all over again. We should approach the strategy not as a set of things to do, but as an orientation for our lives, one that places us in a position to receive power from the Lord. Remember, we can't free ourselves from the grip of the flesh on our own. Most of the work that must be done to release us from our problems is God's work, not ours. He has defeated Satan and sin and death through the work of Christ. By the work of the Holy Spirit he masters our flesh. Our part is to cooperate with his grace.

If we work too hard to get free, our attention once again will focus on the problem. When we cry out with the Christian in Romans, chapter 7, "Wretched man that I am! Who will deliver me from this body of death?" we won't answer, "I will." Or will we? No, only the Lord can free us. Let us present ourselves to him so that he can release us from the grip of problems that we can't overcome.

The books in the Living as a Christian Series can be used effectively in groups. To receive a free copy of the Leader's Guide to this book and the others in the series, send a stamped, self-addressed business envelope to Servant Books, Box 8617, Ann Arbor, Michigan 48107.